Vain Empires

Also by William Logan

POETRY
Sad-faced Men (1982)
Difficulty (1985)
Sullen Weedy Lakes (1988)

CRITICISM
All the Rage (1998)

Vain Empires

◆

p
o
e
m
s

b
y

William Logan

PETERLOO POETS

First published in 1998
by Peterloo Poets
2 Kelly Gardens, Calstock, Cornwall PL18 9SA, U.K.

A catalogue record for this book is available
from the British Library

ISBN 1-871471-52-4

Printed in U.S.A.

FOR RICHARD HOWARD AND DAVID MILCH

lux et veritas

To summer's grate, the firefly's brief glow
adds its dying ember's *caveat*.
Emptor, warn our ancestors, who know
that death, like love, is sometimes dearly bought.

Advise if this be worth
Attempting, or to sit in darkness here
Hatching vain empires.

Paradise Lost

ACKNOWLEDGMENTS

Some of the poems in this collection first appeared in the following publications:

Agni Review: The Advent of Common Law in Littoral Disputes. *Boulevard:* Nativity; The Porcelain Head. *Cambridge Review:* Bar and Grill; Christ among the Moneychangers, 1929; Theodicy of the Air-Pump of Robert Boyle; Tristes Tropiques. *Critical Quarterly:* On the Probation of Coal; Raison d'État; A Version of Pastoral. *Denver Quarterly:* Nocturne Galant. *The Nation:* The Long Weekend; New Year's at the Methodists'. *The New Republic:* Britain without Baedeker. *The New Yorker:* The Shadow-Line. *Paris Review:* Florida Pest Control. *Parnassus:* Keats in India. *Partisan Review:* Chamber Music. *Pequod:* Flower, of Zimbabwe; Lux et Veritas; Masses and Motels. *Poetry:* The Age of Ballroom Dining; Animal Actors on the English Stage after 1642. *Prism International:* 1857; On the Ordination of Women. *Sewanee Review:* The Burning Man; Joachim of Fiore; Joseph Banks and the Board of Longitude; Van Gogh in the Pulpit. *Southwest Review:* Histoire des mentalités; Pears in Solitude; The Plantations of Colonial Jamaica. *Threepenny Review:* NE Seventh Street as the Pequod; The Presence of Evil in Ancient Texts. *Verse:* The Holy Sea; Trouble at the Circe Arms. *Western Humanities Review:* The English out of England; The Long Vacations. *Yale Review:* The Embarrassment of Riches; The Rule of the Rule of Law.

"Robert Grosseteste and the Origins of Experimental Science" was published in *A Garland for Harry Duncan* (W. Thomas Taylor, 1989). "Keats in India" received the 1991 John Masefield Memorial Award from the Poetry Society of America.

These poems could not have been completed without a generous grant from the Ingram Merrill Foundation and a leave of absence from the University of Florida. The University also provided a leave during which the poems were begun and two research grants during their continuation.

CONTENTS

Vain Empires

The Secession of Science from Christian Europe

Many a terrible monster made of broune paper

❖ ❖ ❖

I. ROBERT GROSSESTESTE AND THE ORIGINS OF EXPERIMENTAL SCIENCE

Greek columns, set narrowly against
   the ruptured surface of the Mediterranean,
correct the armies of the declining sun

   where the infant schools of Oxford lie.
To resign all livings for the one
   deception of the senses, as a stubborn bishop

suborns himself to the dignity of the page,
   its ink a gall, its rotted berries coloring
meteors in the human eye and monks

   bending to goatish debaucheries,
proves doctrines concealed in painted capitals
   where ancient snakes devour their tales

and each learnèd smudge repairs an age of truth
   with error. Psalm commentaries couch
their penance in mistranslated passages,

   the glass of wine whose outward surface forms
no inward grace. Gears of the natural world
   turn redemption to revelation, passion to possession

of Western clerks streaming to Constantinople,
   sharpening their pens upon Greek noses.
Take now the advantages of compromise,

the shattering beaker with its poisoned syrup.
On his blunt thumbnail, a mother-of-pearl shard
gleams with prophecies against the Pope.

A man has his meat, and also his prey.

II. THEODICY OF THE AIR-PUMP OF ROBERT BOYLE

The oranges swell within the Age of Reason.
　　Across the rusted screen, pad by silk pad,
the gecko presses claim upon the eye,

　　black heart soaking through its papery skin.
New realms invent new torture, new anatomies
　　that starve the paper from the settling ink,

the fraught wealth turning butchery to science.
　　The status of experiment can change
the psychic fraud to overnight success,

　　live acid seeping through the sewer's cast.
So in his oaken barrel Hooke decompressed.
　　So Boyle stroked his pigeon's ruffled feathers

and laid it in the pump where turn by turn
　　sleek pistons stole the air, while in their chairs
nodding philosophers adjusted their wigs

　　and watched the captive pigeon suffocate.
They feasted on a roasted stack of squab
　　like Englishmen eating raw seagulls in their search

for northwest passage to the Chinese silks.
　　What memory corrodes is not the "art" of knowledge.
The purity of science cannot change

　　the common sins of beakers and retorts,
the broken backs of coal fields conjuring up
　　thin tubes of ether and glass, dead Merlin's spells

transmuting North Sea oil to Armani's smells.

III.   HISTOIRE DES MENTALITÉS

Desire reflects our own translucent eye,
    the white corrupted ball of milky curd
that stares, stares upon shadowed galleries,

    the simple truth, if not the single truth.
A glance cannot repair Goliath's oozing head
    or pull the absent skin, like a slipcover,

over the naked horror of the bronze flayed horse.
    Participation in the divine idea
raises the staining tide beneath the bed,

    drains through rotting casements, down stone steps,
mires the counting room and private court
    where peacocks bicker over a roll of dice.

No one trusts the blank check of the patron,
    his bathrobe some faked thread of tapestry
still moist with indigo. A glass-eyed fly,

    he buzzes around the artist's breathing corpse.
The colors of a conscience cannot mend
    the leaden armature of chiaroscuro:

we cannot see that world in black and white.
    Alas! It's easier to reconcile
our chatter to gilt daubs on plaster walls.

    There's no escape from sensibility.
The shuttered pope at Avignon withdrew
    into the sanctum of his private bath

whose steamy clouds were etched with the will of heaven.

IV. JOSEPH BANKS AND THE BOARD OF LONGITUDE

One might in youth concede to investigate
   such practices of the cod as require the French
to creep within their bark-lined suits

   and split the fish in woolen gloves,
not touching the violet entrails,
   or take ship to observe the transit of Venus,

to crawl along a caterpillar of coast
   where among the fray of moral appetites
vast cabinets might be filled with skins

   as rare as scrolls, and eggs whose translucences
were not inferior to the morning star.
   Bligh suffered for his breadfruit trees,

a nicety not recognized at feasts
   where the tropical Pacific changed to wine
and natives traded frail songbirds wrapped in net

   for the hand-carved crosses of the gods.
These gods take breakfast on the flying fish
   or such idle and unprofitable specimens

as would exempt themselves from human company
   and might enamor the queen who should not *chuse*
to encumber herself with the stuffed animals.

   Against those who in the European disease
would place geometry in distant suns,
   one would rather stand within the homely science

of gears, escapement, of the movement of hands.

V. THE AGE OF BALLROOM DINING

In history's deep thicket, each monster wears
    a mask to hide his face, but the salons
require the formalities of skin

    when dining on the courses of illusion.
They powder their tongues with the essay
    of war, chronic gossip of tragedy:

the amputated limb and punctured eye,
    children gutted in the ditch, great humps
of horses, flies clogging their throats,

    such impersonations of pleasure
as on the stage requite the actor's silence,
    the evening in a candlelit room.

A hunchbacked lawyer rises in argument.
    The hour's contemplations now recruit
the fall of tea leaves from an abandoned jar.

    A maidservant of servants, weeping in the closet,
counts minutes wrung from the mantelpiece
    where Neptune throttles his bronze dolphins

and straddles Time, his slender chariot.
    The flaking mirror wraps gilt faces
to its mordant surface. Like photographs,

    they wake from the dream of ambition.
The sleep of knowledge is long and deep.
    To sleep within the wound of sleep,

they wrap their legs with lace.

VI. THE EMBARRASSMENT OF RICHES

*What call you the Townes name
where Alexander the pig was born?*

The plastered rooms were left to prostitutes
    whose impure sullen skin, like blotting paper,
was thought to draw away the harmful vapors,

    a process known as drying out the plaster.
Communion with the fragrant and the foul
    called down religion from its cleanliness

and wiped the bleeding hands of Lady Macbeth.
    The city that was once the scar of empire
mounted the frail Venetian chandeliers

    fringed red and blue like airmail envelopes.
Over the Tuileries, a headless king
    might still repent the pestilential church,

the galumphing walk of hobbled gardeners.
    And there, amid the lettuce of the faith,
the politician of the knife and fork

    arms for the armageddon of roast beef.
Philosophers have gathered in the hall,
    and from the flaking psoriatic vault,

whose plaster once prepared a winter sky
    of constellations skewed from native orders,
a spidery pendulum descends by wire

    and slowly knocks against the empty bottles
rayed in a circle, now crossing the chalked mark
    dividing ours from theirs, and theirs from nothing.

They drink the vintage wine from paper cups.

VII. CHAMBER MUSIC

The world of physical objects cannot stain
the minor texts our summer nights applaud:
    the firefly's careless shimmer, its Morse code
    of syntax correcting Keats's ode
To Autumn's now tubercular refrain:
There is no mercy where there is no God.

When Dachau's Jews and whores were sacrificed
to Christian sacraments, no Savior dawned
    like a black sun on the Black Sea: the wine
    of old communion kept the dead in line.
The weak fish grappled in the claws of Christ,
the osprey turning from His shattered pond.

We have our music too. It substitutes
the flames of Wagner for the string quartet.
    The violinist cocks his bow, and with a nod
    the bald conductor lifts the hand of God
and dips his black baton. A barren flute
takes quavers from the rage of sunset.

CHRIST AMONG THE MONEYCHANGERS, 1929

Among shivering bankers the coin went false,
and on damp walls the shreds of tapestry
repented the cost of flowers under glass,
the foul pool swollen with fish, small vanities
whose scales were weighed out coolly in silk thread.
The stink of plaster corrupts the polychrome
and carp convert in secret to the cause
of wall-eyed ancestors flaking under crests
now mangy lions rise rampant to protect,
their hair shirts still acrawl with louse and worm.
The raggled matrix of an hour's peace
cannot reform crude factions of a state
never alone except among the mad,
who on their knees vomited up pale blood
that splashed like taxes on the flagstones.
Sumptuous deaths in the shade of politics,
and then the posthumous careers, the charter bus,
the cure of hunting hawks and not their masters.

THE LONG VACATIONS

The honeysuckle raged
upon mossy gardens,
sweetness sickening, beckoning
each time we turned a page

of those musty novels by Scott.
The papery moths thwacked
against a hurricane lamp
even the hurricane forgot.

A nameless lady sold us eggs
from her splay-foot, rickety table
with its tempting pool of change.
Her bantams pecked at our legs

but gave up double yolks
Mother fried for her lunch.
Our tomcat stalked the gulls
while she told dirty jokes.

We were, quite frequently, bored
little children, nasty and cross.
After we left they tried,
for murder, a man we adored.

It's difficult to forget, or forgive
the tedious years in a place.
Someone lives there still.
Someone more sensitive,

perhaps. But who forgave
our childish demands?
Out of eight long summers
there's little left to save.

Why, ancient Mary Soule
who died just a year ago!
She could squeak the exact squeak
of a Baltimore oriole.

New Year's at the Methodists'

That Christmas our lost dinosaur
ruled over Baker's Beach,
whose mutinous sands had mired
the Portuguese men-of-war.

They trailed from old issues of *Life*,
their tentacles filthy, like plastic.
On New Year's Eve we were minded
by the Methodist minister's wife.

Over his battered Ouija
the Reverend Mr. Potts
watched as his overturned cup
spelled out tales of Fiji,

where teams of tattooed rowers
would ferry him upriver
to a hut where the chief of the chiefs
stored his power mowers.

With ritual bowls of Coke
slim maidens would offer their charms
which Potts would politely refuse.
Outside the thermometer broke

at not-so-absolute zero.
Jungle ferns formed on the panes.
In the dream of his own language,
every man's a hero.

But what of Mrs. Potts,
who trolled from her antique dory?
She gave us a bushel of clams
called beauty spots

and stacked her Methodist dollars
in a canvas burial shroud
stuffed behind warped shelves
of mildewed Chaucerian scholars.

THE LONG WEEKEND

When Augustine was plundered of coquina block
my mother dreamed the noise of war away,
Block Island cruises and the doctors' sons

who drank anatomy in lecture rooms
and steeped their hands in death. The family
black-paper scrapbooks leaked their corner mounts,

each snapshot mounted like a Bengal tiger,
and mourned the *fin de siècle* upstairs maid
whose Christian conscience snapped one Christmas Eve.

She bathed away her cares in chimney soot.
My mother wished that summer to be black
and tanned while both her friends stayed lily white.

They fished the southern reaches where the pickerel
regained the outer margins of the lake,
the mirrored blue of deco coffee-tables.

The Lord's avenging angel brought the mail
from Iceland, Normandy, wherever boys
took leases on my mother's high-school charm.

Grandmother's beaded dresses lay embalmed
in dime-store tissue and cedar cabinets,
the past my mother wrapped herself within

while shaking V-mail from its envelopes.
Beneath the past, another past corrupts
all memory of place. My mother found

a numbers runner's box of betting slips
still wedged between the hand-sawn attic joists,
Dutch Masters on the lid. It was her joke,

whenever small disasters made us weep:
Dutch Masters. It must have been Dutch Masters.
She fell asleep one wartime afternoon

and woke to children and the atom bomb.

The undersecretary,
mindful of the sharks,
trails across the lawn
in August's purple darks.

He bears a tray of juleps
with mint fresh from the tins
that circle our white houses,
attracted by our sins.

His wife sings "Rock of Ages,"
emptying the pitcher,
then swings it back and forth
like an acolyte his censer;

the undersecretary
assumes a priestly air
and sprinkles benediction
upon our wicker chairs.

He cuts his little finger,
opening his knife.
I am, he reassures us,
Resurrection and the life,

and measures out the cheese
to fit a slab of bread.
By spring the lane of elms
will be a line of dead.

The crickets in the bindweed
chirp like broken pipes.
Stiffly we sit to pose
for a late daguerreotype,

but darkness now has stolen
the light we need to see
the lines upon our faces
and guilts of property.

We laugh and lift our silver
cups to drink a toast
to sweet Kentucky bourbon,
God, and Emily Post.

THE ADVENT OF COMMON LAW IN LITTORAL PURSUITS

I.

From marshy ditch to ruined copse

to ruined corpse, trained arguments confuse
police with politesse. What shy, cadaverous wreck
has understood the season's misconstruals?
Through the stripped thatch of hedges, harvesters

in white linens root their crops,
but in their horsehair wigs confute
the language of the innocent or mute.
The man who murders on his neighbor's beach

murders his neighbor, but on his blooded sand
claims due right of salvage. The islanders
inhabit an island of regard, correction of an appetite,

and take their lesson from the flight of cranes.
They feed their sea of hunger to the flames.

II.

The oyster's genuflection in the dark
consoles the season's conscience to the grave

denial working past the hour of dawn.
Dark fishermen thread the fish, or fugitive,
home to the fire, while broken buoys cork
the Irish channel, and migrant birds have flown.
A spray of salt slows the rotting crab;

the coil of seaweed construes a lady's purse,
feathering the sand with the gull's brief surprise,
the magistrate of matchstick ribs.

Along the shelf the shattered hulls would mock

the salmon muscling upstream to its source.
Like tourists the broad dunes of October walk
the cloven slate stones and the men-of-war.

NATIVITY

Call the quarter-hour's regard, the thin
tinkling in the knell of the pocket watch!
Upon the knoll a grim burning patch
of flowers flowers the dissolving pain

of winter, and in strict order farms
the stricken waters from their sluggish flow.
Divine peace of shattered frost, the law
sentences the hedgerow's scattered psalms,

storms northward down the weedy lanes of corn.
A vanquished light, vanishing late
by streak and veining to its absolute
vocation, repays their mildness with scorn.

Cold images of slate announcing grace,
upon the table an echo of command.
Grave councillors in their burning mend
their blind advice into the rusting sheaves,

but to what consequence? They will reject
these fiery decorations of the calm,
rejoicing the tattoo within the palm,
a room of six by none, or none by six.

THE WOMAN OUT OF GUYANA

Now every music has an animal impatience.
On their paperclip legs, the herons suffer
a mean illness of the ordinary,

the casual infection of polite motive.
They totter away as if they were yours.
Noli me tangere. Touch me not,

lest I be touched, so Christ to Magdalene.
Pastel cars, pale as Necco wafers,
sweep beneath the crown of palms,

a Polaroid whose flat emulsions favor
the TV's airless vision of extremity.
The southern light

frosts the chalky clapboard houses,
which seem flat, like cardboard houses.
The long white seawall out of Georgetown

beckons, and the faint music of little bands
in their cream whites, and polished brass.
The morning waves have been whipped

into a memory of meringue.
It would be hard to dream of beginnings here,
freed of the church bells' toxic clanging,

far from the wake of the interior.

PEARS IN SOLITUDE

A blackbird vacantly delouses the hedge,
yellow beak pointing like the weathercock,
now west, now east, but having heard

of infestations elsewhere, he takes his leave,
too sadly, perhaps, to be believed.
The weathercock turns his back on us,

and on the slates the last gale cracked.
His old pretense—he's nowhere else to turn.
We turn our backs on him. No matter the weather,

rusty sun or bright scholarly rain,
his sullen demeanor must be maintained.
Even the pears turn inward, according to

the demands of saintly meditation.
Gathered in twos or threes they might
whisper against the apples of South Africa

or unripe limes from the generals of Brazil.
Alone, they cannot contrive
a change—but look! The weather *is* changing.

Those rags of cloud that all afternoon
threatened to wipe the sky with a murderous rain,
the fifth this week, have torn themselves up,

the yellow scraps of forsythia, so savagely pruned,
are blooming in the brushpile, and on the river
mallards argue fluid mechanics.

Now the blackbird is back, mouthing a shred of reed,
a belated peace offering, but not to us
nor to the regal crocus rising from earth.

There's an unsaintly gleam in the weathercock's eye.

FLORIDA PEST CONTROL

The blonde unlocks
her daddy's Firebird,
blood-red as a tropical fish.
Privilege, that old *bête noire*,

shakes its head in her exhaust.
Her rear lights swim
in a fantail's glide.
The South exists,

I write my liberal friends,
with its wage slaves
and Burger King estates
in burning, frivolous pastels.

No one can dream it away,
though plasma centers drain
the blood of black and white,
our ball and chain.

The houses turn to dust
beneath us, gnawed by termite,
beetle, or the fear of God.
Only the past can't be exterminated.

Down the street Christo's men
sheathe a house in red plastic
and pump three days of poison in.
Last year two hapless thieves

broke a lock and wandered through
a termite-ridden house in Tallahassee.
They choked to death
in twenty minutes. Christ!

THE SHADOW-LINE

A shadow loon flies from the glassy lake
over mangroves and the freshwater pond
where a lone canoeist casts between the fronds
lying along the shore like broken rakes.

He shatters the inky lacquer where the stars
are scattered like a pinch of cooking salt
in the old recipes. It's no one's fault.
The red dot on the tree line must be Mars,

or just a radio tower blinking, blinking
messages two lovers might overlook.
Night fish are rising to the maggoty hook.
I can't tell any longer what you are thinking.

The shadow of the loon will soon embrace
the shallows of the continental shelf
as night becomes a shadow of itself.
Another shadow passes over your face.

We used to spend summer nights listening to jazz—
rude subtleties of the horn! Now we discuss
surrendering to what will happen to us,
or ought to, or perhaps already has.

THE SECOND COMING

A dreadful summer on the face of it,
mosquitoes thick through the marshes
and all the cottages stinking

of mildew and charging high prices.
In Milford or New London, I remember
a man spray-painting the shell of a Buick—

the car was green, the withered grass green,
even the man was green,
as if a vegetable goddess had waved her shock of corn

and changed him into a tamarind.
The air conditioning broke down the first day.
Finally we chose to travel all day,

drawing down at sunset to a beach at dead water,
the tarry sand littered with men-of-war,
their lavender sacs beating to the hot breeze.

The air smelled of sea trash
and the sky was pierced by the angry squall of gulls.
Thirty years, and so little had changed!

Barnacles, white as chipped teeth,
gripped the wormy pilings of the wharf.
The Methodist church had been gutted

and the honeysuckle torn to the root.
We stayed at the historic inn, though the service
was unfriendly, and ate from the old menu

that had spoken of a new forgiveness.
The preachers and so forth begged us for money.
The one we had come to see was already dead.

THE PORCELAIN HEAD

November, but last summer
is not yet over,
the moths haven't slacked
their midnight attacks.

You lean into the doorway,
the dry-cleaned edges
of your raglan jacket
cutting a draftsmanlike outline

harder than Degas's.
The dresses of his ballerinas
fray in galleries,
but the bronze smile is intact.

Do you remember the tides
we scoured so painfully in Provincetown,
up early to catch the draining
by the Methodist church?

The pipe stems and marbles
rose Lazarus-like from the sand.
And once, twice, the midget porcelain head
of a bored doll, or a broken arm,

trouvailles for the town-bred archeologist.
The sands of Egypt, Mass., await.
Sphinx, O ruthless Sphinx,
memory is kinder

to archeology than to memory.

THE DEATH OF PLINY THE ELDER

Dear Tacitus, you've asked me to account
for my uncle's death. He was at Misenum then,
commander of the fleet. On the ninth day
before the calends, he was deep in his books
after sunbathing, a freezing plunge, and lunch.
My mother told him of an unusual cloud.
He called for his sandals, waddled uphill, and saw
a ragged mist rising from Vesuvius,
fissured like a great umbrella pine.
High in the air, the trunk had opened out
in spindly branches, some bleached, some marked or
      mottled.
He ordered his men to make a galley ready
and gestured toward me with an invitation;
but I refused to leave my writing chair—
I had a difficult subject to compose.
As he left the house, a note came from Rectina,
the wife of Tascus, whose villa was in danger.
The expedition then became a mission—
the quadriremes were launched, and he set the helm
toward beaches clotted now with fleeing men,
straight into danger, and yet so calm, so cold,
he noted every shifting wisp of smoke
and had his secretary jot them down.

And now the ashes fell into the ships,
heavier, hotter, the nearer they were rowed,
and pumice stone and blackened gravel, scarred
or shattered by the fire. The shallows were blocked
by rubble from the mountain, and they could not land.
The wary helmsman warned him to turn back,
and my uncle hesitated. Then he said,

Fortes fortuna juvat, and on they rowed
around the ashen bay, toward Pomponianus,
whose villa lay in a cove at Stabiae.
On ship Pomponianus had assembled
his oils, money, robes, and manuscripts,
but could not sail against the headlong wind.
Borne on this wind, my uncle reached the shore,
embraced his panicked friend, then asked for a bath—
and after bathing lay down in state to eat
with passion, or at least pretense of passion.
From Mount Vesuvius, broad sheets of flame
and fires flashed, like a baker's open ovens
glaring in the darkened watch of night.
My uncle, to console his friends, insisted
that these were fires in deserted villas.
Then he lay down and slept. His breathing was,
I must say, unmistakable, a throaty growl,
and, being fat, he snored like an instrument—
his friends could hear him, listening by the door.
The courtyard slowly filled with ash and pumice—
he was awakened. (The walls were shifting now
first one way, then another, shock after shock.)
They feared to stay inside, they feared outdoors,
where pumice stone, though porous as bread loaf,
rained down through the ashy air. At last they chose
the deadly rain above the deadly walls,
my uncle moved by reason, his friends by fear.
With linen, they tied pillows to their heads.
Elsewhere day had come; there it was night
(blacker than any ordinary night),
pierced by lamps and torches. Down they stumbled
to the pumice-littered beach, but the black waves

still roared against the ships in angry crests.
My uncle lay on a sailcloth thrown ashore
and called for gouts of water, which he drank
like someone dying of thirst. The running flames,
the smell of sulphur on the air, put all to flight.
My uncle staggered up between two slaves,
but then fell down again, wheezing terribly,
his windpipe blocked by ash and caustic vapor.
When daylight came, they found his rigid body,
no mark upon it, dressed as he was in life,
more like a sleeper than another of the dead.

All through that day my nose was in my books.
I bathed, and dined, and fell into broken sleep.
That night the shocks—so frequent in Campania—
became so violent the world turned over.
I rose. My mother came to my narrow bed,
and in the courtyard we composed ourselves.
I called for a book of ancient history
and started to read, a man without a care.
Now it was dawn, but the early light appeared
so faint and sickly it was hard to see.
The courtyard walls were leaning in upon us—
we couldn't stay; we chose then to escape.
Crowds followed us in panic, like a tide
boiling with maddened fish. Our carts were dragged
clear of the houses, but on the pitching road
not even heavy stones could weigh them down.
The sea had withered up, as if withdrawn
to deep uncharted caverns in the earth.
On the broad flats, sea creatures beached and died—
fish, and monstrous things that flapped like fish,

and others no one could identify.
A black cloud scrabbled from the distant hills,
torn by great tongues of flame. They writhed like eels.
Sometimes yawning in haggard forks of lightning,
soon the black cloud had squatted on the earth,
inking out the sea, and then Misenum's cape.
My mother urged, begged, demanded that I leave her.
Burdened with age and crippled by her weight,
she thought that she must die for me to live.
Gripping her hand, I harried her along—
she followed, with reluctance, through the crowd,
but not without a word of self-reproach.

Now came the ashes, wafery at first.
Behind us, smoke had blossomed in black petals.
I was afraid that in the pitch of darkness
we would be crushed within the weeping mob—
I said we had to reach the open fields.
There we were hooded in darkness, like a shroud,
but not the easy dark of moonless night
or nights of blowing cloud, but dead flat black,
the blackness of sealed rooms unlit by torches.
We heard the cries of women whimpering,
the whinnying of children, cursing men—
they knew each other only by their voices.
Many raised their hands to unknown gods,
but most believed that all the gods were dead.
We were to witness the apocalypse.
A faint glow came—but it was not the dawn,
just fire, fire everywhere behind us.
Then darkness, and ashes rough and coarse as plaster.
At times we had to stand and shake them off

for fear of being smothered by the weight.
My consolation was, I knew we all would die.

But then the darkness weakened and, like smoke
dissolving, blew out in wisps, and daylight broke.
A pale sun rose, as if in deep eclipse.
Before our stricken gaze, the world had changed,
now covered by a layer of ash, like snow.

Van Gogh in the Pulpit

London, 1876.

              I am a stranger on earth,
hide not Thy commandments from me.

                          The pigeons swoon
in volleys round the brick Wesleyan spire.
There is soot, the understanding of soot,
along the vision of the Richmond Road.
The terraces move

              uphill toward grace,
toward the salvation of the ordinary.
And if we look back,

                back into our disgrace,
from which we have made our little progress,
the gray clouds

              are rent chalky and scarlet
like the vestments of the Anglican priest.
The working poor of London live as miners
wrapped in black,

              black-faced along the face of walls
at which they chip,

              chip with leaden hammers.
The gas will flare and scour the streets
here in the heavenly city.

              Our feet shall be sockless
and we shall make our shirts of dry sacking.
We shall be in our normal condition,

              abasement
before the potato eaters,

              black as loam, kneeling

to the soiled foot of the sower,
bending to the harrowed cloth of the reaper,
the broken meat that fleshes the digger's fork.
Expelled from Paradise,
      that will be our paradise.

1857

The *Fleurs du mal* betray the *Fleurs de l'Inde*
Rimbaud would promise *Une Saison en enfer.*
In these and other versions we have sinned.

Her sailors brought to France the tamarind
that graced the hothouse garden's jardinière,
but *Fleurs du mal* betray the *Fleurs de l'Inde.*

L'Orientalisme's fading wind
gabbles at the gaslight like a prayer.
In these and other versions we have sinned.

The public gardens grow undisciplined.
Traduttore traditore, declare
the *Fleurs du mal* but not the *Fleurs de l'Inde.*

Read Proust, Verlaine, or Mallarmé, chagrined
by all such orchids suffer unaware
of these and other versions. We have sinned

each time a word of ours has helped rescind
the privilege of lies. Or words of theirs.
The *Fleurs du mal* betray the *Fleurs de l'Inde.*
In these and other versions we have sinned.

BRITAIN WITHOUT BAEDEKER

I.

From the shell's contrary run and the gull's

sugary distemper, the river cannot cover
the metalled road that like a wedding band
binds the college causeway to dry land.
The mint and salt grass taint the winter light:

its slow refusal of the vacant nests
turns toward the island like a rough caress
the idea that all of love is property
and property is merely appetite.
The starving birds along the Backs have begged

raw gobbets from the coughing tourist's leg

and through their mouths the icy figures burn.
Beyond the fen the dead elms queue for spring,
which follows our cold fever with saws and fire.

II.

The dunnock and reed warbler brood the lone
survivor whose gross beak outgrows his home
until the summer breaks the cuckold from his word

and spreads the voices: drifting, brutal, absurd.

JOACHIM OF FIORE

The figure rises from gold template and border,
filigree of haloed saints swanning
the influence of the Holy Spirit

and yet submissive to the will of Rome.
The pilgrim swarms cannot impede
your flight into the wilderness,

Eternal Evangels burnt in revelation,
or heretics chained beneath the railway station.
The gospel will not guard the moral pass

nor gild the colored fragments of a triptych.
The Pope has swollen with your additions—
such mathematics of the dead, twice dead,

wall up the Church's paper-thin partitions.
No more the concord of a testament,
the democratic church of mendicants

barefoot in the snow of dogma, healed
by that regarding light of faith and hope.
But who will gather in a room whose false

illuminations scour the crumbling plaster?
Can those grim lepers who were saved
be bandaged in the scripture of refusal,

their characters corrupt, corrupting,
lest even these return upon their masters
and strangle them within their feathered sleep?

The heralds of new age descend to blow
tin trumpets in the deaf ears of the damned;
the watery sun rises from the trembling east

over the lost magi, the lesser, the least.

TRISTES TROPIQUES

The nuance of the palm trees
    abuses the regret
of careworn Romeo
    and his fat Juliet
who have outgrown their teenage
    suicide pacts.
Death comes turning the page
    and death is just the facts.

We lose our moral beauty,
    grow sensitive to smells.
The gift shoppe's jewelry boxes
    are glazed with broken shells.
A blood-stained mattress dries
    in the Vacancy Motel.
Life is no version of living.
    Life is just hell.

At night the tourists gather
    beneath the winter moon.
It has a bad complexion.
    It will be waning soon.
Learning how to die
    is finally just an art,
says the shopping mall
    to the shopping cart.

Nocturne Galant

She stalked like a goddess on carpet
through our two-star rented room,
indifferent to her bare bottom
or the cruelties of perfume

that drifted up from the whores
who kissed on the neon walk
the Marines who gave nothing but money
and got nothing back but talk.

Our argument lasted till midnight,
the right of it nothing but wrong.
I laughed in my borrowed tuxedo.
She cried into her sarong.

True love would climb the Himalayas
or drink the Amazon dry
and promise to promise forever
but never ask a girl why

true love has the tongue of a tyrant
who makes the traitor confess
to treasons he has not committed.
The poet knows little or less.

And no one remembers the reasons,
the boring and terminal sighs,
the casualties of inbreeding,
the crocodile tears in her eyes.

I promised her that I'd be faithful
with all my faithless heart
for a month or until next Tuesday.
Love lies, and so does art.

To the Orthodox Ambassadors

I. THE RULE OF THE RULE OF LAW

The stork who for his murders was not crowned
haunts the curve of garden walk that leads
   to gray interiors, bank balances,

   and cocktails by the fruit trees lopped of fruit.
Those who live under dispensations of good
   promise laughter at the trial, the private joke

   at the hanging. And yet the air,
damp as a dishcloth, covers the raggled lawn,
   chary witness to the lavishing gloom,

   eager auditor behind the plough.
The light shuts down behind the terraces.
   The thick waist of convenient fashion

   surrenders neither conscience nor control,
ancestors who sliced the vein of marriage
   to undertake the cures of property,

   the pleatings of money or its dispositions.
What midnight whispers by dawn is published abroad:
   the Court of St. James will ignore

   his dripping necklace measuring a throat,
her alligators drifting through the grove.
   The blood that falls upon such heads repays

   such sanctity, such boredom, such cigarettes.

II. THE ENGLISH OUT OF ENGLAND

He who has breathed the temporal powers
    of the great seal of state, the mocking
clamor of the corridors in Peking,
    its pleasure alleys, the smiles of its whore,

finds an island of justice in a world of slaves.
    The clack of typewriters decent in their stalls,
the rush fans wheezing over silent wills,
    cannot judge the scalpel in the autoclave.

And what of the murdered sprawled beneath
    economies of speech, the harmless gesture
in politics of trade or polite rupture?
    They measure no obituary, no wreath.

The small breasts of his mistress will still impart
    crude fantasies to the office boys,
the steam yachts flee the mirrored bays,
    each rented sunset seem a work of art.

III. THE PLANTATIONS OF COLONIAL JAMAICA

Praise the narrow waters of religion
closed as a dolphin's mouth, or dauphin's skull.
The benefits of slavery will not accrue

to mocking gargoyles of corrosive lime,
the shudder in horse latitudes
at the steady drip of dysentery below,

the tidal diplomacy of miasmic mists.
Mornings the priest opens his arms to the Host,
lifting the gold-plated chalice like a soccer ball,

eyes on the angels' just system of labor.
His hymns to the failing plantations
of the Lord, the starved soil of indebtedness,

console the wounded innocence of the snake
twining around stained columns
in distant banks, in courts of mixed commission

where wigged defenders gather at a cough.
We live within the act of ritual,
wearing the salvage of a banished cotton,

such light burdens whipped between lost continents.
The myriad saints, rejoicing in the knives of flame,
found in the corruption of fire

an adequate repentance for empty desire.

BAR & GRILL

The evening blackboard flared
with scribbled strokes of chalk
and drops the size of olives
split open on the walk

before a BAR & G ILL
whose neon sign's disease
lit pink formica tables
and menus glazed with grease.

Two dripping brokers shook
out handkerchiefs of silk
and leaned their *Wall Street Journals*
against the sour milk

that curdled in their coffee
and wished that it were cream.
A chalk-white businessman
awoke from a nervous dream,

rose from his plastic placemat
and curled up on the floor.
The Puerto Rican waitress
burst through the swinging door.

She fanned his face with a menu.
The owner beat on his chest,
while the rest of the diner watched
in stunned disinterest.

Over the cooling coffee,
each faced his own estrangement.
Alone I went to meet
a previous engagement.

ACADEMIC FANTASIA

I. N. E. SEVENTH STREET AS THE PEQUOD

Across the street the children
   go down to the burning stream.
The cardinals are dreaming.
   The cabbage palms are dreams.

The blue FOR SALE signs have
   marooned the iron fence
whose iron spikes harpoon
   the night's long violence

and wrapped around the clothesline
   the bedsheets serve as shrouds
to wind around the sleeper
   whose TV dreams too loud.

The ship's corroded anchor
   knocks against the door
that raps out our block captain,
   Ahab the realtor.

His white-finned Cadillac
   is difficult to steer.
Its patchwork paint suggests
   the brickwork of Vermeer

or other sharks that swim
   beneath the streetlight's shrewd
opinion of the streets,
   our common latitude.

Across the street the children
　　lie in the burning stream.
The cabbage palms are dreaming.
　　The cardinals are dreams.

II. TROUBLE AT THE CIRCE ARMS

Some small-town temptress might
   appear incognita
and lure to bars the boys
   from Troy or Ithaca

and under neon teach
   them vintages of wine.
By midnight she could turn
   the frat boys into swine.

No leader will undo
   their taste for history's swill.
They study every night
   the freedom of the will.

Their faculties cannot
   dispute the tenure of
the sty's fraternities,
   such animals of love,

but here the scholar pigs
   erect a plaster saint,
expecting to receive
   her courses in complaint.

The Greeks who would forget
   stare blindly at the sea
of white noise on their screens
   and *Lotus 1-2-3!*

THE REFORM OF ANTIQUE GOVERNMENT

I. ON THE PROBATION OF COAL

Those muddy embargoes that precede
the steam heating of public houses,
monthly farrowing interest in the straw,

collect appreciations like overdue accounts.
The faces narrow to a needle vein,
a grimace that clings to pickaxe and pole,

limed carcass among the rotting soils:
hollow galleries ease down their rails.
The voiceless deaf cannot inherit

a lattice of roses steadying the estate
or houses silking into gardens
and gardenias. Fires in the counting room

warm the cloisters' symptomatic dissolution,
diseases like the charms of penitence
scattering through basement and bonfire.

The old works' low combustion heats
young ladies from their paragraphs
and gentlemen stringing houses up

on swinish mortgages, obscene instruments
to boil hair from grimy bodies.
Elsewhere the market of routine requires

spring cabbage or onion edging the formal maze,
the rootled nodules of potatoes,
pasteboard tickets to a local terminus.

Blackberries gather their canes near wharves,
the martial convenience of a native shore's
profusion of slag gardens or rank hills.

II. ON THE ORDINATION OF WOMEN

Like a dog's walking on his hinder legs

The dark comes on in damning silhouettes.
The falcon and the hunter's rig conspire
along the roads that fear has organized

and those who lie down in speech by cold waters
will find compassion passion's substitute.
To become mere idea behind the nave

where traitorous families blind their sons
in the barber-pole shades of cassock and cotta,
barking behind their wrists, would carve

concession from the grand Concessionaire.
The old pretenders hover in sackcloth and ashes,
begging absolution for the Absolute.

To followers the poisoned leaders pass,
consorts of the shielded eye, harriers of the ear,
of the tongue's displacement, the hand's thwarted housing.

The wafer settles within dry mouths,
and choirboys chorus their satisfactions
down the clumsy corridors of the throat:

Sir, it is not done well; but you are surprized
to find it done at all. The orison
delivered by an unnamed priest: *Ordaining you*

would be like ordaining a dog or a potato.

III. ON THE PRESENCE OF EVIL IN ANCIENT TEXTS

To take from alien languages
the prosecutor's thou, the infected I,
invites from clay tablets the Old Enemy,

winged enormity beyond the hillocky grave,
aesthete of the quarterly and the cabinet.
Through the landau window half-lit clouds

scud the broken pines, where the hot breath
of the horned dragon might supersede
our understanding of evil. What a connoisseur

one must be of his presence! The license
God grants suffering and the Fall,
the little inflections of sadism,

franchises of capital for the believer
who cannot see the drab ordinariness
of chaos. A broad and fiery sunset eases

into the turquoise mosaic of the bay,
spawning the scarred Leviathan
now watermarked on the stationery of accountants.

The systematic carnal lie, the long
plagued decade in the house of derision and grace,
argues the mocked reversal of a private life.

Whitman: *I was on Arch and Chestnut Streets—*
such crowds—oceans of women, drest to kill—
every kind of article you can think of,

& many you never thought of.
Permit these isolates their ecstatic seclusion,
their enemies the consolation of folding money.

The old satisfactions, the least endearing.

Two Religious Caterpillars

I. THE HOLY SEA

The proposition of palms implies a rare
    theater of original disgrace
where manatees diminish their returns
    and each aspiring shark must hide his face.

No male receives the bitter envelope
    that nature tenders to the insincere
without first making an off-color joke
    blaspheming the celestial Engineer.

The Guidebook's unoriginal remark
    will echo down the hallways of the damned
and no flamingo in the pink will wear
    his papal robes without a monogram.

II. MASSES AND MOTELS

The strangest dogma has the strongest smell.
Our bishop of the Virgin Birth declares
his burning hatred of the heretic
but takes communion from the French *au pair*
    whose catholic
desires serve a sacred clientele.

Alone, the drabbest parson makes obscene
gestures that condemn *The Faerie Queene*
but whets his congregation's appetite
with nightmare visions from the magazines
    that would ignite
love, if love were soaked in gasoline.

The cows asleep beneath the pollarded oaks
content themselves and would not misconstrue
the country vicar longing to have sinned
with choirboys upon medieval pews.
    A sudden wind
fills out the blossom with short strokes.

THE BURNING MAN

At length he comforted the criminal
town councillor or priest, but women chiefly,
   caught in the flytrap of the Renaissance,

the rack's *Malleus Maleficarum*
   on whose thick slats the marriage vows were spat
to heresy's familiars, nine dead cats

   hung drooling from a wooden altarpiece
to mock the crucifixion of our Lord.
   And neither water nor a cooling cloth

was he allowed for their relief, knowing
   the word of God afflicts the innocent
no less than white-hot bars applied by grace

   to heal the lying tongue, the perjured eye,
or drive the seven crippled demons from
   the weakened anus or the vaginal tract.

Two hundred in two years, conducted to
   the final mercy of the brush and stake,
the youngest under nine, a pair of sisters

   who clung to one another in the flames,
a blinded girl whose trembling hand he took,
   and others too numerous or dead to name

or afterwards recall as other than
   a blackened face, a cage of blackened bone,
both those who on the rack confessed their sins

and those who still protested innocence,
since none could suffer such exquisite hurt
　　without the devil's bland conspiracy.

Their screams reminded him of childbirth,
　　their pleas for death that rose to nightmare shrieks
as their dresses caught and drifted up in crumbs

　　of glowing ash. More terrible than these,
the laughter of the crowd that warmed its hands
　　and later pissed upon the glaring coals,

the stink of burning hair, the incomplete
　　cremation of the flesh, which hung in strips
across the smoking corpse like ribbons of beef

　　suspended from the crossbars of the smokehouse.
The scent of roasting women was a rare perfume
　　to noses cottoned by the stench of shit

flowing through gutters, or the fragrant worm
　　that danced from rotting flesh and took its lease
in pages of corrupt Gregorian chants.

　　Happy the corpse, because it is dead;
much happier the tortured, still alive;
　　more fortunate than either, the unborn child

who has not heard our names or seen our hands.
　　Took solace from the wounded and the sick,
and nursed the suppurations of the plague

when hand-drawn carts drew off the freshly dead
to shallow lime pit or the burning trench.
    The fever burned beneath his whitened skin,

his penitential moans like tallow candles
    melting with plague, the straw bed hot with fleas
that took his last confession, though his tongue

    had swollen like a steer's, his swaddled groin
attained the rank consistency of cheese.
    Despite his protests, argued in the full

Aquinian logic of a Latin doubt,
    and published in the double-columned fonts
that like the Wehrmacht wheeled through provinces,

    the murdered would have sentenced him to sit
in the dock of the accused at Nuremberg
    with those who knew but did not dare to speak;

with those who spoke, but did not dare to act;
    with those who might have acted, but did not;
with Auschwitz doctors and the Dachau whore.

Animal Actors on the English Stage after 1642

Now the dog all this while sheds not a tear

Bearwards, ape-leaders, owners of trick horses,
down the long vans from Africa and the north
the stunned survivors of the Inns of Court
in frenzied howls accepted empty purses,

knowing they were guilty of high treason.
Still those who unrepentant had returned
beneath the smoking boughs of lime trees burned
by fleeing royalists, their long hair chastened

seditiously in curls, at these banned houses
in humble standing offered to besiege
their dream within the drama of the stage,
though Cromwell's ass just muttered empty phrases:

a ravaged bear, fresh-baited at pit, staggers
toward the benches howling for Prince Hal,
the monkey shaved in motley plays the Fool,
Macbeth's three bulldogs sheathe their bloody daggers.

RAISON D'ÉTAT

The daffodils have pierced the crust of April
like spears gripped in the hands of Roman soldiers
still buried in the fenland's ancient marshes

where ravens starved of corpses tear each other.
Decay can never penetrate the bodies
of soldiers who have fallen in the marshes

or morning papers casually recording
that in a dusty Middle Eastern schoolroom
a man was wired naked to a chair back,

his legs spread open like a pregnant woman's
to let a boyish Christian flare his lighter
again and again upon the prisoner's skin

while outside dirty children heard his screams.
The soldiers failed to gain what information
had led them to the village and the schoolroom.

In England there are villages and schoolrooms
where children learn by rote the information
that king by king will pass examinations

while yellowed charts display their fathers' empire
whose altered names by rote they have remembered,
the climate, population, and chief products,

the photographs of charming native customs:
the doctors stand in feathers and regalia,
the chieftains cure incurable diseases.

They are not taught the politics of reason,
why doctors in their white coats gently handle
the sleeping prisoners they've strapped to gurneys

to ease into their arms the sterile needles
and drain each body of its quarts of blood.
The blood is shipped to save the lives of soldiers

who are not soldiers but are school-age children
sent unarmed to clear paths through enemy minefields,
to lie across the ribbons of barbed wire

and let their bodies serve the feet of others
who fly like cuckoos to nests of machine guns
where if they die they die official martyrs

who in their heaven will be singing warriors
and will not need the sterile bags of blood.
The doctors now are running out of needles.

FLOWER, OF ZIMBABWE

They dined Thursdays in the Army and Navy Club,
whose porter—it was a House of Commons joke—
was more distinguished than the oldest member.
Two old-school types, one almost cancerous.
The gaunt one lit his old-school pipe, and gazed
into the crystal tumbler of his horse's neck,
then pulled a paper cutting from his pocket.
"His name was Kenneth Flower, damn fine chap—
ran agents from the grass huts of South Africa
through Mozambique, before Mugabe shook
our school chums from their office suites, if not
their suits. Thought nothing of judicious murder,
as casual as slapping a mosquito—
once bribed a bush priest with Afrikaner gold
to ship his students to guerrilla camps,
recruits for Zanu-PF. But there's the rub—
Ken kitted them out in poisoned uniforms.
the chemical pregnation of the cloth
leached slowly through their skin, and in the grass
they stiffened for the vultures, not the Church.
It couldn't last—the deaths seemed damn suspicious.
To tidy up Ken shot the bloody priest,
who never twigged that Flower was the head
of state security, which bugged his nave
and buggered him in the apse, you might well say.
Guerrillas blamed each other, and Flower turned
his coat the day Mugabe was sworn in
and served the blacks with equal diligence.
He had a bit of a giggle, don't you think?"

The fat one nodded, and waved his cigarette:
"You had to know your Ovid in those days."

KEATS IN INDIA

1848

Just as the sun went down, the monstrous bats,
fatter than crows, with tissue-paper wings,
unloosed their hooks from the thick and stringy palms
and calmly sailed around us through the dusk.
They pillaged the garden mangoes, lumpy as fists,
which tasted of apricots smeared with turpentine.
We'd shut up all the windows to keep cool—
the air was gravelike, but an open door
blazed like a furnace mouth at Colebrook Dale.

Next morning we embarked by the Burning Ghât,
a ground as deep as a squalid London square.
Each cluttered hut of straw and spit, leaning
against a leaning wall of powdery brick,
encased a sickly Hindu like a shell.
Along the water's edge, the funeral pyres
smoke and sweat, and finally exhaust
the little tepees of sticks that families
have gathered there. I saw two bodies burning,
frizzling really, and giving off a smell,
the old familiar sweet and fetid stench
that reeked our clothing in dissecting rooms.
Above the walls the hurgilas comport,
half-stork, half-vulture, stiff and sorrowful
as village undertakers. We call them adjutants—
they pose as motionless as marble statues
until their meals are cooked. The carcasses,
like fresh-baked bread, steam in the morning air,
and when the wood has sputtered out are pitched
upon the tide, floating miserably

back to the shore, or blindly setting out
along the sacred Ganges to the sea.
The hurgilas flap out, perch awkwardly
upon their breasts, and tear the roasted flesh.
The sick who will procrastinate their deaths
are dragged down to the river, where relatives
fill up their open mouths with sacred mud.

We had engaged a frayed Bengali pinnace
of sixteen oars, decked over with bamboo,
the low, light fabrication of our cabin
just slashed bamboo and straw, a rumpled cottage
without a chimney, much less a chimney pot.
The boatmen crouching above us on a grate
stirred the dark water with their bamboo oars,
long stalks tacked at the end with rounded boards.
The river flattened like a sheet of paper,
rice grounds on either side, softly animate
with the calls of white and scarlet paddybirds,
each homely village masked with blossoming fruit,
like scenes of Oxfordshire along the Thames!
The dirt floors of the houses swarmed with frogs
as plump as goslings, speckled green and black.
The boatmen now were towing us with ropes
against the current, their limbs and backs
grown scaly from their hourly immersions.
They used to swim aboard like water rats
when porpoises larked around our sluggish passage.
We grounded on an island made of sand,
bordered by reeds and curling grass—ashore,
we came upon the fresh prints of a tiger
prowling beneath a gibbet where two men,
almost reduced to skeletons, were hung

in chains. Its feet were large as dinner plates.
At sandy Sibnibashi we were plagued
when clouds of hideous insects clogged our candles,
some burning away their wings on the glass shades,
others flying straight into the craters
to meet a waxy death. We paid no heed
to what next day became a ghastly spectacle,
the army that was fluttering on the ceiling,
wet with paint, and clung there black and stinking
until the ants devoured them. The ants,
my close companions in this airless cabin,
have shared the moldy store of my provisions,
and, as if to save me from my own complaints,
they've eaten up a box of bluish pills.
Some fakirs swam aside to beg for alms,
but one stood on the bank, a raw-boned man
like Shakespeare's Edgar topped with a filthy turban,
a mad array of rags and wretchedness,
two satchels flung across his narrow shoulders,
the shredded length of a scarlet cummerbund,
a palmetto leaf he held like a lady's fan
and which he waved as he stood laughing at us.

Dacca was the wreck of ancient grandeur,
its castles, mosques, and dainty palaces,
the factories and churches of the Dutch
all sinking into ruin, were overgrown
with snaky vines and bushes of the jungul.
The palace court now hosts a tiger hunt—
it was here we were unwilling witness to
the practice of suttee. A bamboo stage,
so low and meanly built, is roped together
and the body then prepared in state upon it.

The widow is led out and stretched beneath,
surrounded with brush or twiggy combustibles—
they have to drug the younger girls with wine.
Pressed down with long bamboos, she starts to cry
as ghee is poured upon her. It flares like resin
when the solemn relatives ignite the stage.
Her whining screams are terrible to hear.

We came to a drowning country, cheerless marsh
and seas of reeds, but briskly on we sailed
like a greyhound through a field of broken corn.
The alligators swam all evening round our boat,
lifting their long black snouts in friendliness,
except a monster, fifteen feet in length,
striped black and yellow like a garden wasp.
We passed a herd of swimming cows, the cowman
towing himself by their hips and hairy tails
and guiding the Judas cow with a broken staff.
A smartly bangled, hennaed country woman
came quietly down to bathe at Mongyr Ghât.
She stepped in with her mantle wrapped about her,
with decency and seemly modesty,
and as the river rose beyond her breast
she squatted underneath—so long I thought
nothing could save her. And only then she rose,
and walked like a goddess up the dusty path.
The distant Greeks, I almost am convinced,
long followed similar custom—how otherwise
could clinging pleats of sodden drapery
have entertained—entranced!—the ancient sculptor?
Later that day we saw a murderer.
One of the sailors, bathing by himself,
spied through the reeds a fakir strangle a man

and bury him in the sand. We passed the spot
and saw the fakir washing bloody clothes,
but we were far from the authorities,
who probably would have taken little notice—
the thuggees, who we thought had been suppressed,
are said to promise to their goddess Kali
an offering of lives, like English tithes.
We might have shot him with impunity.

We landed in Benares, holy city—
the building stone from Chunar, fine and pale,
is smeared with deep-red paint, then populated
with elephants, with gods and goddesses,
with women, men, white bulls, and flowerpots!
The sacred bulls of Siva, tame as mastiffs,
walk sleepily up and down the narrow streets,
and lying down can hardly be kicked up.
There is a stinking, templed monkey garden,
sacred to the ape who conquered old Ceylon—
its denizens are fat and ripely orange.
They creep out to the fruiterers and dine
impertinently on the wares, or snatch
rich gobs from the mouths of children at their meals.
An Englishman was drowned last year in the Ganges
for having shot at one in ignorance.
We saw a few examples of the penance
where holy men distort their arms or legs
by posing them for years in one position,
or clench their hands until the curling nails
grow out the backs. We saw a dancing cow.
The astronomical observatory,
thought ancient and now crumbling into ruin,
still has a course of lectures. Prim young men

in spectacles, fast sweating through their suits,
produced a coarsely painted plaster globe
and waved their hands beneath the southern pole
where they supposed the sacred tortoise squats.
And this a Government establishment!
They showed the sun sail gaily round the Earth
as if they lived in Alexandria
and I were Ptolemy. The pilgrims come
down the broad steps, where thousands of both sexes
are occupied in bathing, where merchants hawk
their wares beneath the shade of gay umbrellas.
The pilgrims buy two pots, called kedgerees,
and tying themselves between them paddle out
to the center of the stream, sit bobbing there,
then tip the pots until they fill with water
and sink into eternities of rest.
I wish that death were always thus obliging,
and sold the pots that promised our salvation.

We now proceeded overland by horse,
our servants armed with spears and hammered swords.
The camels followed like a caravan!
The country from Allahabad is jungul,
uncultivated, flat and wild, broken
by marsh, impassable in rain. Poor Wordsworth
I think would button up his collar and huff
at all these casual miles, no walk in sight,
and scarcely a bush to make a figure of.
We have to wrap our heads in turban cloth
while our bearers try to whistle up a wind,
like English sailors. The sun has blistered us,
though it has froze at night, and the shade chills.
My servant is insensible to weather—

he sleeps all night on the gharry's open roof
while we catch shivers in the smoky carriage.
One night I brought a blanket up to him,
and asked next morning whether it gave him comfort.
"Oh very, sir," he said. "It was my pillow."
Half down a bank, there lay an elephant,
groaning, groaning, a mountain of flesh and bone.
We gave the wretched animal a cordial,
but all the bearers could not raise it up.
It haunted me the long slow miles to Lucknow.
At last the iron bridge across the Goomtee
rusted before us. Our horses steamed and snuffled,
clacking their iron shoes. The muddy river
ran sullenly below, and on its banks
a few white figures worked with sticks, stirring
the dusty smell of India, like barley.
Across the river, there were the domes of Lucknow,
like gems within a chalk of dazzling white,
the buildings knocking one against another
down miles of riverbank, and each one more
majestic, airy, stranger than his neighbor,
while scores of minarets, pale spiky needles
taller than Nelson's column, pierced the dry air
with a twisting, frightening grace not of this world.
Each burning dome was crowned with burnished gold.
I stopped the horse and leaned against the view—
the glare of Indian sun shimmered around us.
The ground itself became a polished mirror,
and there was the dream, the dream of fairyland.
At last, I thought, at last I have been taken
into the Orient's magnificence.

We rode like princes into India's mirage,
but as we rode, the vision thinned and wavered.
The distant, starry color of the buildings,
serene Italian marble in the sun,
up close was whitewash, peeling, fly-blown.
The marbled walls were only stuccoed brick,
and the gilded domes, the perfect draftsman's arcs
as massy as St. Paul's, were shells of wood
in many places rotten, roosts for doves
murmuring and flaring out in dusty clouds.
You come at last to the conclusion,
the city of your dreams is but a fraud.
For half a mile we threaded narrow streets,
filthy lanes between the crowded houses,
crossing once a handsome avenue
wider than Oxford High Street, with Gothic buildings
the same pale oyster—I might never have left.
The mazes opened into a paved square
with a large and dingy, now deserted palace
used as a market, and there amid the trash
an elephantine gateway, Room-ee-Durwázu,
the most complacent arch I'd ever seen.
Room-ee-Durwázu, called the Gate of Rome,
by which they mean Constantinopolis.
Like Alexander, there I was at last,
come continents to face the long road home.
I have begun the "Ode to Darkness" now.

Notes

The Secession of Science from Christian Europe

The epigraph is a phrase of Stephen Gosson's, from *Playes Confuted in Five Actions*, and refers to the Elizabethan stage. Robert Grosseteste was the Bishop of Lincoln from 1235 to 1253. He had a remarkable range of philosophic and scientific interest and lived to a great age. The title of the Grosseteste section is the title of a book by A. C. Crombie.

In "Theodicy of the Air-Pump of Robert Boyle," reference is made to one of Boyle's favorite parlor tricks, the suffocation of a pigeon by the creation of a partial vacuum. The scene was the subject of a well-known painting by Joseph Wright of Derby. The scientist Robert Hooke decompressed himself in a barrel in 1671.

Joseph Banks, the eighteenth-century English naturalist, observed the transit of Venus with Cook in Tahiti and was later a member of the board that deliberated over the difficult problem of calculating longitude at sea. The queen was Queen Charlotte, consort of George III; the stuffed animals, seized by the Royal Navy from a French expedition, were eventually acquired by the British Museum. I have taken some details and at least one phrase from Peter Campbell's review of *Joseph Banks: A Life*, by Patrick O'Brian (*London Review of Books*, 7 May 1987).

The Long Vacations

Mary Soule ran a little candy store and cleaned the two-room schoolhouse in the coastal village where I grew up.

The Long Weekend

The old Spanish fort at St. Augustine is built of blocks of coquina, a material composed of fragments of marine shells and coral. It was effective in absorbing enemy cannonballs. In World War II, the Army microfilmed soldiers' letters to save cargo space; back home, they were printed full-size on photographic paper. This was called V-mail (V for Victory).

The Advent of Common Law in Littoral Pursuits

The egg case of the skate, often seen along beaches in tangles of seaweed, is called a "lady's purse."

Florida Pest Control

To kill termites, exterminators in Florida build a tent of plastic sheets around an infested house and pump in gas. Among the gases favored are sulfuryl fluoride and methyl bromide, though tear gas is added as a warning agent. Signs with the skull and crossbones are posted outside.

The Death of Pliny the Elder

This is a slightly condensed version of two of Pliny the Younger's letters (Book VI: xvi and xx). Except in the matter of one proper name, I have followed the old Loeb Library edition, and I have at times borrowed phrases, I hope judiciously, from prose translations by William Melmoth (as revised by W. M. L. Hutchinson for the Loeb edition) and Joseph Jay Deiss (from his book *Herculaneum*). *Fortes fortuna juvat* = Fortune favors the brave.

Van Gogh in the Pulpit

Van Gogh preached a sermon in the Methodist Wesleyan Chapel in Richmond, near London, on 29 October 1876.

1857

The year of publication of *Fleurs du mal* also saw the publication of an anthology titled *Fleurs de l'Inde*, which I found in a Cambridge bookshop.

Joachim of Fiore

Joachim of Fiore, a Calabrian abbot who died in 1202, believed that the age of the Father and the age of the Son were to be followed by an age of the Holy Spirit. His influential prophetic works were widely misused. See Marjorie Reeves and Warwick Gould, *Joachim of Fiore and the Myth of the Eternal Evangel in the Nineteenth Century*.

To the Orthodox Ambassadors

In Britain, terraces are groups of houses with a brick facade and party walls.

Academic Fantasia

The Circe Arms was the name of an apartment building in Gainesville. For the purposes of the poem, I have translated it to somewhere in upstate New York, along the rough line of cities named for classical sites: Ithaca, Syracuse, Rome, Utica, Troy.

The Reform of Antique Government

In "On the Probation of Coal," it may be important to know that in Britain, on occasion, a coal mine (there called a coal pit) will catch fire and smolder or burn for generations.

In "On the Ordination of Women," the epigraph and first quotation are Samuel Johnson's. The second quotation comes from an article in *The* (London) *Sunday Times* (6 July 1986).

"On the Presence of Evil in Ancient Texts" includes some lines from a letter Whitman wrote on 22 February 1881.

The Burning Man

Malleus Maleficarum ("The Hammer of Witches") was used as a text during the witch hunts in Europe. The poem is based on the life of Friedrich Spee von Langenfeld (1591–1635), a scholar and priest who served as confessor to the condemned. He was probably present during their interrogation under torture. He later repented his role and wrote a book (*Cautio Criminalis*) that exposed the madness of vengeance and corruption at the heart of the trials. He died of the plague at Trier while nursing the sick.

Animal Actors on the English Stage after 1642

In 1642 the Puritans closed the English theaters. The title and the first line were suggested by Louis B. Wright's "Animal Actors on the English Stage before 1642," *PMLA* 42 (1927), 656–669. The line about Cromwell derives from the information, noted by Wright, that in the Chester play *Balaam and Balak* Balaam's ass has a speaking part of fourteen lines.

Raison d'État

The poem is based on incidents reported in news articles about southern Lebanon and Iran during times of war. In Iran, one method of executing political prisoners was to have doctors anaesthetize them and then drain their bodies of blood.

Flower, of Zimbabwe

The Army and Navy Club is in London, and a horse's neck is a drink. The details of Flower's career derive from a review of his autobiography, *Serving Secretly*, in *TLS* (13–19 November 1987). Zanu-PF was Robert Mugabe's guerrilla organization

I have allowed the gaunt speaker to skew one or two of the facts.

Keats in India

The year before he died, Keats thought of taking a position as surgeon on an Indiaman and "voyaging to and from India for a few years." He went some way with this fancy before giving it up. See his letters to Miss Jeffrey on 31 May and 9 June 1819, as well as the letter to his sister on the latter date. His letter to Dilke in May 1820 shows that he had not completely abandoned the idea. The poem supposes that Keats survived his tuberculosis and later settled in a quiet way in India, able to afford a somewhat romantic river journey up the Ganges in 1848, when steamships would have made the rowing and hauling old-fashioned. The poem is indebted to the memoirs of Robert Minturn, Harriet Tytler, and particularly Reginald Heber, from which lines and phrases have been taken. The hurgila, also known as the adjutant bird, is a stork that sometimes grows to a height of seven feet. Jungul (also jangal or jungel, in addition to our more familiar spelling) was originally uncultivated waste ground, covered with shrubs or long grass. Only after the word had entered English did it receive its modern sense. A gharry is here an enclosed carriage, though sometimes it simply refers to a cart.

I have no doubt taken ideas, and perhaps a phrase or two, from other books and articles. Let this serve as acknowledgment, however inadequate, of my borrowing.

WILLIAM LOGAN

is the author of three previous collections of poetry: *Sad-faced Men* (1982), *Difficulty* (1985), and *Sullen Weedy Lakes* (1988). His collection of essays and reviews, *All the Rage,* has been published by the University of Michigan. William Logan has received the Peter I. B. Lavan Younger Poets Award from the Academy of American Poets and the Citation for Excellence in Reviewing from the National Book Critics Circle. He teaches at the University of Florida, where he is Alumni/æ Professor of English. He lives in Florida and in Cambridge, England.